Henrietta

Katharine Stanley-Brown Abbott

Illustrations by
Kristin Richland

Henrietta, published February, 2022

Editorial and proofreading services: Taylor Morris, Karen Grennan
Interior layout and cover design: Howard Johnson
Illustrations: Kristin Richland
Photo Credits: Illustrator photo © Mary Claire Carroll of Carroll Photos

Published by SDP Publishing, an imprint of SDP Publishing Solutions, LLC.

All rights reserved. No part of the material protected by this copyright notice may be reproduced or utilized in any form or by any means, electronic or mechanical, including photocopying, recording, or by any information storage and retrieval system, without written permission from the copyright owner.

The characters, events, institutions, and organizations in this book are strictly fictional. Any apparent resemblance to any person, alive or dead, or to actual events is entirely coincidental.

To obtain permission(s) to use material from this work, please submit a written request to:

SDP Publishing
Permissions Department
PO Box 26, East Bridgewater, MA 02333
or email your request to info@SDPPublishing.com.

ISBN-13 (print): 978-1-7378019-7-9
ISBN-13 (e-book): 978-1-7378019-8-6

Copyright © 2022, Katharine Stanley-Brown Abbott

Printed in the United States of America

This book is dedicated to everyone who discovers that they are braver than they thought they could be.

ACKNOWLEDGMENTS

When I saw a little woodchuck nibbling lettuce in my vegetable garden, this story nearly wrote itself. After our successful collaboration on *A Zoo Full of Rhymes* in 2020, my daughter Alexandra and I returned to SDP Publishing. Again, we were happy to work with Lisa Akoury-Ross and her talented team who provided professional expertise and sensitivity to our vision. Kristin Richland, whose enchanting illustrations highlighted my rhymes last year, agreed to illustrate *Henrietta* and we are immensely grateful. My family has all provided enthusiastic encouragement and helpful advice. I am particularly grateful that my daughter Victoria made thoughtful suggestions that helped me rework the story for the appropriate-aged audience. Most of all, my heartfelt thanks are for Alexandra. This is the third book she and I have published together and she has mastered liaison with SDP Publishing, handled all the production activities, and coordinated the art work. Without her knowledge, perseverance, and attention to detail, this book would still be just a manuscript. Henrietta is Alexandra's book as well as mine.

Henrietta, a curious woodchuck, poked her brown, furry head out of her burrow and looked around. She watched as a little girl tugged at some green leaves, pulled a red ball out of the soil, and wiped the dirt off it. Henrietta heard a snap as the little girl took a bite. She thought that sounded exciting and decided to try it herself. Whatever it was, it would make a nice change from her usual diet of dandelions, clover and alfalfa.

When the girl left, Henrietta scurried over to the garden. Using her paws she pulled at the green leaves until a red ball popped out of the ground. She wiped it off as she'd seen the little girl do and took a bite. Ooh! Her mouth burned. It was too spicy so she spit it out. However, in the next row, there were long green stems with shiny sacks hanging from them. Inside the sacks were little green balls. They were sweet and delicious. Henrietta ate as many of them as she could reach.

The next day she heard a woman say, "Someone has eaten all the peas."

"It wasn't me, Mom," said the girl. "I just ate a few radishes. But I did see a woodchuck in the yard."

"That's the answer, Lily. Woodchucks like vegetables."

That afternoon Henrietta went back to the garden and nibbled some bright green leaves. They were soft and smelled earthy. Suddenly the woman rushed out to the garden, clapped her hands and shouted, "Go away! Don't eat that lettuce!" Frightened, Henrietta scurried off to her burrow. She was puzzled. If the little girl could eat the red things, why couldn't she eat the green things?

The next day, curiosity got the better of Henrietta and she went back to the vegetable garden. Right next to the garden was a big box with shiny metal mesh sides. Henrietta could see that it was full of pretty green leaves that looked like the ones she had eaten the day before, and those were very tasty. The box was open, so Henrietta padded in and began to nibble what was inside. Suddenly she heard a sharp click, and the door to the box slammed shut.

Henrietta didn't pay much attention to the noise because she was having a lovely time eating what was in the box. But after she'd eaten all the greens she decided it was time to go back to her burrow.

She tried to paw at the latch to open the door, but it wouldn't budge. "I can't get out of this box and it's getting dark. What will I do? It's cold in here. I wish I was back in my burrow, all warm and cozy." She tried the latch again but it wouldn't open. Henrietta was scared, but then she thought at least she was safe in the box. Even if she couldn't get out, no other animal could get in. Not knowing what else to do, she curled up in one corner of the trap and tried to sleep. But there were strange noises, like owls hooting, and scuffling in the grass. At one point she thought she saw two dark eyes staring at her from outside. She could hear some animal enjoying a midnight meal of vegetables. Henrietta was so scared her body shook and sleep was impossible. "Oh, I wish I'd never gone into this box, but those green things looked so delicious."

In the middle of the night, it started to rain. By morning, Henrietta was cold and shivering. "I'm miserable, I'm hungry, and I want to go home."

Lily and her mother came out the next morning to check on the garden. When Lily looked in the trap, she saw the soaking wet woodchuck with its head hanging down. The lettuce and parsley were gone. Lily's mother looked at her garden. "Oh no," she cried. "All my zucchini has been eaten."

"It couldn't have been the woodchuck," said Lily, "because it's in the trap. Just look at that poor little thing. It looks so unhappy. Can't we let it out?"

"It ate all my peas and lettuce," said the girl's mother crossly.

"But not the zucchini. I think we should let it out," said Lily, "before it catches a cold. Please, Mom?"

Reluctantly, her mother agreed. They opened the trap door and watched Henrietta scurry off to her burrow, shaking herself as she ran. Henrietta was happy to be out of the trap. The little girl had been very nice, but the woman was really cross. What could she do to show them that she was sorry? She wouldn't eat any more of the woman's vegetables. But that didn't seem like enough. Then she had an idea.

That afternoon when the sun came out, Henrietta went back to the vegetable garden and stood by the pea vines. Soon, two chipmunks came near her. Remembering how the woman had clapped her hands to scare her off, Henrietta batted her paws together and squeaked at the chipmunks. Startled, they ran away.

Henrietta clapped her paws and squeaked at a squirrel who fled before it could snatch a cherry tomato. She even waved her paws to scare away a determined blue jay. All afternoon, Henrietta stood firm guarding the vegetables.

Every day Lily watched the woodchuck standing in the vegetable garden. It didn't eat any of the vegetables and made sure that no animals or birds did either.

One afternoon, a red fox appeared. It wasn't interested in eating the vegetables—it wanted to eat Henrietta, who stood next to the cherry tomatoes. She didn't see the fox at first. With its head lowered and thinking of a tasty meal, the fox crept closer. Henrietta spotted it and began to shiver. In spite of feeling terrified, she stood by the tomatoes, but wondered if she could ever escape. All she could do was squeak and that didn't scare the fox.

Lily was sweeping the kitchen floor and happened to look out the window. She was horrified to see a fox, baring its teeth, creeping toward the little woodchuck. Realizing the woodchuck was no match for a fox, Lily knew she had to save her brave friend. She ran out the kitchen door waving the broom and shouting, "Go away, get out of the garden and don't come back." She shook the broom at the fox, who slunk away as fast as it could. Henrietta was still shaking but the little girl knelt down and said, "You were very brave to stand still but you're safe now." Henrietta was so happy that the little girl had saved her that she jumped up and down before dashing across the lawn and diving into her burrow.

Seeing how brave Henrietta had been, Lily decided the little woodchuck deserved a reward.

"You know, Mom, the woodchuck could have been eaten by that fox, but it stood there guarding our vegetables. I think it's showing us that it's sorry for eating the peas and lettuce. We should give it a thank you present."

"I'm going to have our garden fenced in next spring so the woodchuck won't have to stand guard. Perhaps that's a reward," answered her mother.

"I have something else in mind," said Lily, "but it's a surprise for next summer." She made her plan, studied seed catalogues and, when nobody was around, did the necessary work. By spring everything was ready.

When Henrietta woke up from her long winter's nap, she saw a little vegetable garden near her burrow. Green vines circled wooden stakes, and mounds of soft green leaves peeped out of the soil.

Across the lawn, Henrietta saw the little girl and woman she remembered from the year before.

They stopped in front of the garden. "Here's my surprise for that brave woodchuck," said Lily. "I've planted a garden just for it with peas, lettuce, and even zucchini."

Henrietta looked at the garden. Everything that was sprouting looked delicious. She was so happy she jumped up and down. "Isn't this a nice reward for extraordinary bravery?" said Lily to her mother. "Yes, dear," answered her mother. "Your reward is perfect."

Lily watered the garden every day. She was happy to see Henrietta guarding her vegetables and, when they ripened, nibbling them. Lily's mother was happy that no animals ate her peas, cherry tomatoes, lettuce, or zucchini.

But happiest of all was Henrietta, the little woodchuck who had discovered how brave she really could be.

ABOUT THE AUTHOR

KATHARINE STANLEY-BROWN ABBOTT is an editor for newspapers, and newsletters, as well as the writer of two memoirs, three cookbooks, and a commemorative book for a women's social club. She is also the author of *Cobblestones and Ice Cream Cones—A Trip to Nantucket in Rhymes* (2019) and *A Zoo Full of Rhymes* (2020).

She considers herself a generalist. Her eclectic interests include needlepoint, knitting, cooking, travel, reading, tennis and life-long volunteerism. She is also an accomplished collage artist whose work has been exhibited and sold in juried shows, art festivals, and open studios.

Abbott is a graduate of Vassar College, the mother of four adult children, and grandmother to five grandchildren. She is widowed and a resident of Manchester, Massachusetts. Find out more at her website: *glassheadbooks.com*

ABOUT THE ILLUSTRATOR

A native of Vermont, **KRISTIN RICHLAND** is fascinated with animals and our natural world. She enjoys taking liberties mixing them up, playing with archetypes and slipping in little nods to fairy tales and lore.

Richland is a graduate of the Maine College of Art's painting program, and was a professional picture framer for many years before switching to the world of bookselling.

This is the third book she has illustrated, and her second collaboration with Katharine Stanley-Brown Abbott; the first being *A Zoo Full of Rhymes*. Her artwork can be seen in several Vermont galleries, and at *Kristinrichland.com*.

Henrietta

Katharine Stanley-Brown Abbott

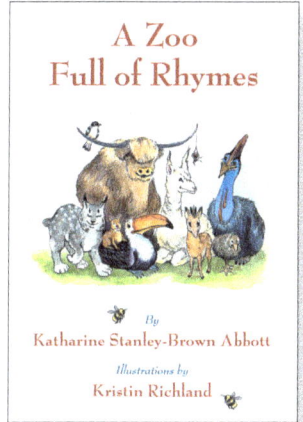

Also by the author:

A Zoo Full of Rhymes

www.glassheadbooks.com

Publisher: SDP Publishing

Also available in ebook format

www.SDPPublishing.com
Contact us at: info@SDPPublishing.com

CPSIA information can be obtained
at www.ICGtesting.com
Printed in the USA
BVHW021208040522
636097BV00013B/104